Simple G Eclipse

Practical Guide

V. Telman

Practical Guide

1.Introduction

What is Eclipse?

Eclipse is a versatile Integrated Development Environment (IDE) designed to be modular, extensible, and flexible. Initially conceived primarily for Java development, Eclipse has rapidly evolved over the years into a universal platform that supports many other programming languages and technologies through the installation of plugins. Thanks to its plugin-based architecture, Eclipse can be utilized for developing applications in languages such as C, C++, Python, PHP, JavaScript, and many others.

The versatility of Eclipse is also reflected in its use across various development contexts: it is widely employed for web, desktop, and mobile application development, as well as for advanced software engineering projects, embedded systems development, and even academic research.

Eclipse's user interface offers a range of features including a sophisticated code editor, debugging tools, an integrated version control system, project management tools, and much more. With its vast ecosystem of plugins, developers, teams, and companies can customize Eclipse to precisely fit their needs. The environment allows working on multiple projects simultaneously, featuring various views, editors, and functionalities that make the development cycle more efficient and organized.

History of Eclipse

The Beginnings

Eclipse was born in the early 2000s as an IBM project. Before Eclipse, IBM was using a tool called VisualAge for Java for internal software development and for its clients. VisualAge for Java was considered a powerful development tool, but it had a monolithic structure that made it difficult to extend and adapt to the new needs emerging in the software world. To address this issue, IBM decided to develop a completely modular development environment, extensible through plugins and, most importantly, open source. Thus, in November 2001, IBM announced the release of Eclipse as an open-source project, and with it, created the Eclipse Foundation, a community to manage the ongoing development of the platform.

The name "Eclipse" was chosen because it symbolized the intention to "eclipse" Sun Microsystems, then the leading company in the Java development tools sector thanks to its IDE, NetBeans.

Evolution and Growth

Eclipse quickly gained popularity, not only for its use as a Java IDE but also for its ability to add plugins to support other languages and technologies. In 2004, the Eclipse Foundation was officially established as an independent, non-profit organization tasked with managing and coordinating the development of the platform. The creation of the foundation represented a crucial step in establishing Eclipse's neutrality and fostering open collaboration among various companies in the tech sector.

In the following years, Eclipse became a universal development platform. Numerous stable versions were released, each introducing improvements and new features, making it a more comprehensive and competitive environment. With the expansion of its plugin ecosystem, Eclipse began to be used in non-traditional software development areas, such as modeling, scientific research, and embedded device development.

Eclipse Today

Today, Eclipse is one of the most widely used IDEs in the world, with a vast community of developers and companies supporting it. Its modular architecture and the flexibility it offers remain its strong points. The Eclipse Foundation continues to oversee not only the Eclipse IDE but also a range of related projects spanning from the Internet of Things (IoT) to artificial intelligence, making Eclipse a fundamental pillar in the landscape of open-source software development.

One of its most recent innovations is Eclipse Theia, a web-based IDE platform that aims to replicate and surpass Eclipse's capabilities in cloud environments, seeking to usher the development experience into a new era.

Advantages of Using Eclipse

Eclipse offers numerous advantages over other IDEs, making it a popular choice for developers of varying experience levels and business sectors.

1. **Modularity and Extensibility**

One of Eclipse's main advantages is its plugin-based architecture. This means that users can customize the development environment based on specific needs. There are thousands of plugins available for Eclipse, ranging from version control integration (like Git and SVN) to those for specific programming languages (C, Python, Ruby, PHP, etc.). This flexibility allows for creating a tailored environment that meets the specific needs of any project.

2. **Multi-language Support**

Although Eclipse was initially designed to support Java, it now supports a wide range of programming languages. The IDE can be configured to work with languages such as C, C++, PHP, JavaScript, Python, Ruby, and many more. This makes it an ideal choice for those working on projects involving multiple languages or technologies.

3. **Open Source and Free**

As an open-source project, Eclipse is completely free. This makes it an ideal solution for students, startups, or freelance developers who want access to high-quality tools without incurring significant costs. Additionally, being open-source ensures that Eclipse can be continuously improved by a global community of developers.

4. **Extensive Plugin Ecosystem**

The vast plugin ecosystem is one of Eclipse's greatest strengths. This allows users to integrate numerous tools within the IDE, such as advanced debugging tools, integrations with version control systems, code refactoring tools, and much more. Furthermore, companies can develop their own custom plugins to tailor Eclipse to their specific needs.

5. **Large Community and Documentation**

Eclipse boasts a vast community of users and developers. This means it is easy to find online resources such as tutorials, guides, support forums, and more. Additionally, the Eclipse Foundation and other contributors provide detailed and up-to-date documentation to help users get the most out of the platform.

6. **Debugging and Refactoring Tools**

Eclipse provides powerful and intuitive debugging tools that allow for easy identification and correction of errors and issues in code. Refactoring features are also well-developed, allowing for the safe and error-free restructuring of existing code. These tools help maintain code quality and improve developer productivity.

7. **Integration with Project Management Tools**

Eclipse offers native integration with numerous project management and version control tools, such as Git, Subversion (SVN), and other source code management systems. This enables teams to collaborate effectively, manage code changes, and facilitate continuous integration.

8. **Regular Updates**

Eclipse receives regular updates from the community and the Eclipse Foundation. Each year, a new stable version is released with improvements and new features, along with security updates. This ensures that the IDE remains current and competitive with emerging technologies.

Installing Eclipse

System Requirements

Before proceeding with the installation of Eclipse, it's important to ensure that your system meets the minimum requirements necessary for the IDE to function properly. Below are the minimum and recommended requirements:

Operating System

- Windows: Windows 10 or later

- macOS: macOS 10.14 (Mojave) or later

- Linux: Recent Linux distributions such as Ubuntu, Fedora, Debian, CentOS

Java Runtime Environment (JRE)

Eclipse requires a Java Runtime Environment (JRE) to function, as it is written in Java. It is recommended to install a recent version of JDK (Java Development Kit), which includes the JRE.

- Minimum JDK version: JDK 11 (for the latest versions of Eclipse)

- Recommended version: JDK 17 or higher

Hardware

- Processor: Multi-core Intel or AMD, with a speed of at least 2 GHz (a quad-core processor is recommended)

- RAM: Minimum 4 GB, recommended 8 GB

or more

- Disk Space: 300 MB for the basic installation of Eclipse, but additional space is needed for projects, plugins, and external libraries.

- Graphics Card: No specific requirements, but a discrete graphics card can enhance the visual experience in graphical applications.

Download and Configuration

The installation process for Eclipse is relatively straightforward, but it may vary slightly depending on the operating system used.

Steps for Downloading and Installing

1. **Access the Official Eclipse Website**

   To download the latest version of Eclipse, visit the official website at eclipse.org. On the homepage, there will be a button to download Eclipse.

2. **Select the Version**

Eclipse offers different versions based on the type of development you intend to do. You can choose from:

- Eclipse IDE for Java Developers: for Java application development.

- Eclipse IDE for C/C++ Developers: for C and C++ development.

- Eclipse IDE for Web Developers: for web application development with HTML, CSS, JavaScript, and related technologies.

- Eclipse for PHP Developers: for PHP development.

3. **Download the Installer**

After selecting the desired version, a download of an executable file will begin to install Eclipse.

4. **Launch the Installer**

Once the installer file has been downloaded, launch it. The installer will guide the user through the installation process, offering options to customize the installation path and select additional components.

5. **Initial Configuration**

After installation, when starting Eclipse for the first time, you will be prompted to configure a "workspace." The workspace is a local directory where projects will be saved. You can select a default path or choose a custom directory.

Installing Plugins

One of the key aspects that makes Eclipse versatile and powerful is the ability to install plugins to expand its functionalities. Here's a step-by-step guide for installing plugins:

1. **Access the Marketplace**

To search for and install new plugins, open Eclipse and go to Help > Eclipse Marketplace. The Eclipse Marketplace is a centralized repository where you can search for and install thousands of plugins.

2. **Search for the Plugin**

In the Marketplace window, you can search for the desired plugin using keywords. For example, if you want to install a plugin for Python development, simply search for "Python" in the search field.

3. **Installation**

Once you find the desired plugin, click on Install. Eclipse will automatically download and install the plugin.

4. **Restart Eclipse**

After the plugin installation, it is often necessary to restart Eclipse for the changes to take effect. Eclipse will automatically prompt you to restart the IDE after a plugin installation.

5. **Plugin Configuration**

Some plugins require initial configuration. After restarting, follow the specific instructions for the plugin to configure it correctly

.

Eclipse offers a flexible and powerful platform for developers of all specializations, enabling the management of projects of any complexity thanks to its modular architecture and extensive plugin ecosystem. The installation is simple, and once properly configured, it can become an invaluable tool for improving productivity and efficiency in software development.

2.Eclipse Interface

The Eclipse interface is one of the most important aspects of the development environment, offering a combination of powerful and flexible tools designed to facilitate developers' work. Eclipse is a modular IDE that allows configuration and customization of its interface based on the specific needs of each user or project. Its structure of windows, panels, and views may seem complex at first, but it becomes intuitive once the basic functionalities are understood.

The Eclipse user interface is primarily composed of:

- **Editor Area**: The central part of the screen where code is written and modified.

- **Views**: Support windows that provide additional information, such as the project structure, output console, and compilation errors.

- **Perspectives**: Predefined layouts in Eclipse that offer a set of specific views and tools for a certain type of activity (e.g., Java development, debugging, etc.).

- **Toolbars and Menus**: Toolbars and menus provide quick access to the most common features.

Editor Area

The editor area is the central part of the Eclipse interface where developers write and modify code. This space can be used to work on source code files, XML documents, HTML files, CSS stylesheets, and many other supported file types. Eclipse supports **syntax highlighting**, which marks up the source code based on the programming language, improving readability and helping to quickly identify errors or code structures.

When working on multiple files simultaneously, Eclipse organizes editors in **tabs**. Each tab represents an open file and can be closed, reordered, or moved within the editor area. This enables efficient management of complex projects with multiple files and classes.

Eclipse also supports **code auto-completion**, suggesting variables, methods, and classes while typing. This feature is especially useful for avoiding errors and saving time during code writing.

Views

Views are windows that offer additional information or support to developers, such as the project structure or the output console. Views can be moved, resized, and closed based on the user's needs. Some common examples of views include:

- **Project Explorer**: Displays the project's file structure, showing source files, libraries, packages, etc.

- **Outline**: Provides a tree view of the code structure, showing classes, methods, and variables defined in the open file.

- **Console**: Shows the output of running programs and any runtime or compilation errors.

- **Problems**: Lists errors and warnings detected in the project, allowing easy navigation and resolution.

Perspectives

Perspectives are predefined layouts in the Eclipse interface that provide a set of views and tools specific to a certain type of activity. Each perspective is designed to optimize the user interface based on context. For example, the Java Development Perspective offers tools for writing code, running tests, and navigating between packages, while the Debug Perspective provides tools for stepping through code, monitoring variables, and managing breakpoints.

Some of the most common perspectives include:

- **Java Perspective**: The default perspective for Java development. It provides access to the Project Explorer, Java code editor, console, and Outline view.

- **Debug Perspective**: Designed for debugging, it allows monitoring variables, managing breakpoints, and navigating through threads and stack traces.

- **Git Perspective**: Used for interacting with Git repositories, it allows managing code versioning, performing commits, pushes, pulls, and resolving conflicts.

- **Java EE Perspective**: For developing Java Enterprise applications, with specific tools for managing servers, databases, and web services.

You can switch between perspectives using the **Window > Perspective > Open Perspective** menu or by clicking on the perspective icon located in the top right corner of the interface. Perspectives can be customized and saved to match each user's preferences.

Toolbars and Menus

The Eclipse toolbar and menus offer quick access to many useful features. The main toolbar, located at the top of the interface, contains buttons for common operations like:

- **Save** (`Ctrl + S`)

- **Run Program** (`Run`)

- **Debug**

- **Project Navigation**

- **Adding New Files and Classes**

In addition to the main toolbar, there are **dropdown menus** that allow access to advanced functionalities. For example, the **File** menu lets you open new projects, save and close files, while the **Window** menu lets you manage views and perspectives in the IDE.

Editor Customization

One of Eclipse's great advantages is its ability to customize the editor to fit the developer's preferences. The interface offers a wide range of options to improve productivity and make the environment more comfortable for the user.

1. Changing the Theme

Eclipse allows you to change the editor theme to enhance the visual appearance and readability of the code. There are several options to choose from, including a light and a dark theme, which is popular among developers.

To change the editor theme:

- Go to **Window > Preferences**.

- In the Preferences window, select **General > Appearance**.

- Here you can select your preferred theme (e.g., "Dark" for a dark theme or "Light" for a light theme).

- Click **Apply and Close** to apply the selected theme.

Additionally, you can modify the syntax coloring for each programming language. This allows further customization of the code's appearance. To do so:

- Go to **Window > Preferences**.

- Select **Java > Editor > Syntax Coloring** (or the language you're using).

- Here you can change the colors for various syntax elements like keywords, comments, strings, etc.

2. Enabling Code Auto-Completion and Suggestions

One of Eclipse's most powerful features is code auto-completion. This function suggests methods, variables, and classes based on what you're typing. Auto-completion can be enabled or disabled according to your preferences and can also be customized to show suggestions in more detail.

To enable or configure auto-completion:

- Go to **Window > Preferences**.

- Select **Java > Editor > Content Assist**.

- Here you can configure when and how suggestions should be shown, such as setting keyboard shortcuts to trigger auto-completion (the default is `Ctrl + Space`).

3. Font and Text Size

Changing the font and text size can improve readability and reduce eye strain during long coding sessions. To modify the font and text size in the editor:

- Go to **Window > Preferences**.

- Select **General > Appearance > Colors and Fonts**.

- Expand the **Basic** section and select **Text Font**.

- Here you can choose your preferred font type and size.

4. Enabling the Maximum Line Length Guide

In many projects, it is helpful to display a visual guide that indicates the maximum line length (often set to 80 or 120 characters). Eclipse allows you to enable this guide to help comply with coding standards.

To enable the line length guide:

- Go to **Window > Preferences**.

- Select **General > Editors > Text Editors**.

- Here you'll find the **Show Print Margin** option. Enable it and set the desired column (e.g., 80 or 120).

5. Configuring Code Formatting Preferences

Eclipse allows you to configure code formatting rules to ensure consistency among team members or comply with corporate coding standards. You can configure how Eclipse handles indentation, spacing, bracket placement, and more.

To configure the code format:

- Go to **Window > Preferences**.

- Select **Java > Code Style > Formatter**.

- Here you can choose a default formatting style or create a custom one by selecting **New** and configuring each aspect of the format.

3. Projects in Eclipse

Projects are the core of Eclipse. The Eclipse Integrated Development Environment (IDE) is used by developers worldwide to manage and work on a wide range of programming languages, with projects ranging from simple Java applications to complex software systems, including web development, embedded systems, mobile apps, and more.

In this context, a "project" is a collection of source files, libraries, configurations, and resources that form the working unit the IDE interacts with. Each project has a defined and organized structure so that Eclipse can efficiently perform compilation, testing, execution, and debugging operations.

Creating a New Project

Creating a new project in Eclipse is one of the first essential steps to start developing with this platform. The process for creating a project slightly varies depending on the project type (Java, C++, PHP, etc.), but the general logic is similar for most languages supported by Eclipse.

Steps to Create a Java Project

Since Eclipse is widely used for developing Java applications, let's look at how to create a new Java project in Eclipse. These steps can easily be adapted for other types of projects by simply selecting a different project type during the creation process.

1. **Launching the Eclipse IDE**

Once you launch Eclipse, you'll be presented with a workspace. The workspace is the folder where Eclipse stores all the project files, settings, and configuration data. You can create projects in a specific workspace or a different location on your system.

2. **Creating a New Java Project**

- Go to the **File** menu in the top menu bar and select **New > Java Project**.

- Alternatively, you can right-click in the **Project Explorer** window, choose **New**, and then select **Java Project**.

3. **Configuring the Project**

In the "New Java Project" dialog, you'll need to configure some basic options for your project:

- **Project Name**: Provide a meaningful name for the project. Eclipse will use this name to create a directory in the workspace.

- **Project Layout**: You can decide whether to organize the source files and output files into separate folders or combine everything into a single folder. The most common choice is to keep the source files (`src`) separate from the compiled output files (`bin`).

- **JRE**: Eclipse allows you to choose which Java Runtime Environment (JRE) to use for the project. Usually, the default system JRE is sufficient, but you can specify a particular version of Java if needed.

   - **Project Properties**: You can also specify build options, additional libraries, or external dependencies that the project might require.

4. **Completing the Creation**

   After configuring all the options, click **Finish**. Eclipse will automatically create the basic structure of the project and open the **Java Perspective** view, optimized for Java development.

At this point, you'll see the project listed in the **Project Explorer** with a structure resembling the following:

```
JavaProject/
   src/
```

    (no source files yet)

    JRE System Library [JavaSE-1.8] (or the chosen JRE version)

    Referenced Libraries

```
```

Creating Other Types of Projects

Eclipse isn't just an IDE for Java. It supports many languages through the installation of specific plugins. Creating a project for languages such as **C++**, **Python**, **PHP**, or **JavaScript** follows a similar process:

1. **File > New > Other...**

If the desired project type isn't directly available under **New**, select **Other** to access a complete list of project templates. Here, you can choose the desired category, such as "C++", "Python", or "Web", based on the installed plugins.

2. **Configuring the Project**

Similar to creating a Java project, each project type will have its specific set of configurations. For example, for a C++ project, you'll need to choose the compiler, while for a PHP project, you must configure a local or remote PHP server.

3. **Completion**

Once the project is configured, Eclipse will generate the corresponding project structure, similar to the Java project structure described earlier.

Adding Classes or Source Files

After creating the project, the next step is to add classes or source files. To do this:

1. Right-click on the **src** folder (or

another source folder for non-Java projects) in the **Project Explorer**.

2. Select **New > Class** (or the corresponding file type, such as **File** for C/C++, **Script** for Python, etc.).

3. Fill in the file details, such as the class or file name, and click **Finish**.

Eclipse will automatically generate a basic source code file with a predefined structure, such as a Java class with a `main` method or an empty class ready to be populated with code.

Importing Existing Projects

In addition to creating new projects, Eclipse also makes it easy to import existing projects. This is especially useful when working in teams or when continuing to work on a project that was developed on another system or environment.

Importing an Existing Java Project

To import a Java project or any other existing Eclipse project:

1. **Open the File Menu**

   Go to **File > Import...**. This will open the **Import Wizard** dialog.

2. **Select the Import Type**

   In the dialog, select **General > Existing Projects into Workspace**, then click **Next**. This option is what you need if the project has already been set up as an Eclipse project and is located on another computer or another location in the file system.

3. **Select the Project Location**

   In the next screen, you can choose to import the project from a local directory or directly from a ZIP archive. If the project is in a folder on your disk:

- Select **Select root directory** and then click **Browse** to find the project folder.

- If you have the project in a ZIP file, select **Select archive file** and specify the archive's path.

4. **Detection and Import**

After selecting the directory or archive, Eclipse will automatically attempt to detect all projects in that location. If multiple projects are detected, you can select which ones to import.

5. **Completing the Import**

Click **Finish**. The project will be imported into the current workspace and will appear in the **Project Explorer**.

Importing Projects from Git or Other Version Control Repositories

Many developers work on projects residing in Git repositories or other version control systems like SVN. Eclipse provides built-in tools to interact with these repositories and import projects from them.

1. **Installing Git or SVN Tools**

If you're using Git or SVN and don't already have the necessary plugin installed, you can do so via the **Eclipse Marketplace**:

- Go to **Help > Eclipse Marketplace**.

- Search for **EGit** (for Git) or **Subversive** (for SVN) and install the plugin.

- Restart Eclipse to complete the installation.

2. **Importing a Project from Git**

Once the Git plugin is installed, you can import projects from a Git repository:

- Go to **File > Import**.

- Select **Git > Projects from Git** and click **Next**.

- Select the **Clone URI** option to clone a remote repository. Enter the Git repository URL and any necessary credentials.

- Select the branches to clone, then Eclipse will clone the repository and guide you through the process of importing the project into the workspace.

Importing Maven Projects

Eclipse also natively supports **Maven** projects, which are used to manage dependencies and build configurations in Java projects. Importing a Maven project is simple:

1. **File > Import...**

   Select **Maven > Existing Maven Projects**.

2. **Select the Directory**

   Navigate to the directory where the project's `pom.xml` file is located. Eclipse will use this file to import the project structure and dependencies.

3. **Click Finish**

   Eclipse will import the project and automatically download all the dependencies defined in the `pom.xml` file.

Creating, importing, and managing projects in Eclipse is a highly customizable and scalable process, suitable for both small individual projects and large-scale collaborative development systems. With its ability to handle a wide range of languages and environments, Eclipse continues to be one of the most appreciated tools in the software development community.

4. Editing Code in Eclipse and Debugging

Eclipse IDE (Integrated Development Environment) is one of the most widely used tools by developers due to its versatility, efficiency, and broad range of features. The code editor is the core of the development experience, and Eclipse offers a rich environment with tools that facilitate editing, navigation, and code organization, while providing helpful suggestions and functionalities to speed up workflow.

Editor Features

Eclipse's code editor is highly functional and offers a wide variety of tools to enhance productivity. Here are some of the key features it provides:

1. **Syntax Highlighting**

Eclipse's editor supports language recognition and uses **syntax coloring** to make code more readable. Different parts of the code, such as keywords, comments, strings, and variables, are highlighted in different colors, making it easier to understand at a glance.

2. **Code Auto-completion**

One of Eclipse's most appreciated features is **code auto-completion**. As you type, Eclipse automatically suggests keywords, method names, variables, and classes relevant to the context. This not only speeds up code writing but also reduces the risk of syntax errors or typos.

For example, when you begin typing a method name in a class, Eclipse will suggest all available methods with that prefix:

```java
System.out.p // suggests "println()"
```

3. **Code Refactoring**

Eclipse includes powerful **refactoring** tools that allow you to rename variables, methods, classes, and interfaces without breaking the code. Eclipse automatically applies changes across all affected files, maintaining project consistency.

Examples of refactoring operations:

- Rename a variable or method (Shift + Alt + R)

- Extract a method (Shift + Alt + M)

- Move a class to another package

4. **Quick Navigation**

The editor offers tools for quick navigation within the project. Some examples include:

- **F3** to go to a method or variable declaration.

- **Ctrl + Shift + R** to quickly open a file in the project.

- **Ctrl + O** to view the structure of the current file and quickly navigate between methods and variables.

5. **Commenting and Uncommenting Code**

Commenting parts of code is essential for making it more readable or temporarily disabling portions of it. In Eclipse, you can easily comment or uncomment code using:

- **Ctrl + /** to comment with "//"

- **Ctrl + Shift + /** to comment out a block of code with `/* */`.

6. **Real-time Error Handling**

Eclipse flags syntax and compilation errors directly in the editor in real time. A red squiggly line appears under the error, along with a cross icon in the sidebar. Hovering over the error provides suggested quick fixes.

7. **Code Templates**

Eclipse supports **code templates**, which are small predefined code snippets. For example, if you type "for" and press **Ctrl + Space**, Eclipse will suggest several predefined "for" loop structures that you can quickly insert.

8. **Support for Other Languages**

While Eclipse is primarily known for Java development, the editor supports a wide range of programming languages via plugins, including C++, Python, PHP, JavaScript, and many more.

Shortcuts and Code Suggestions

Keyboard shortcuts are an excellent way to speed up your workflow and improve productivity. Eclipse offers a wide range of shortcuts to simplify common operations.

1. **Quick Code Navigation**

- **F3**: Go to the declaration of a variable, method, or class.

- **Ctrl + O**: Show the structure of the current file, including methods and fields.

- **Ctrl + T**: Display a class hierarchy, allowing you to see superclasses and subclasses.

2. **Quick Editing**

- **Ctrl + Space**: Trigger code auto-completion.

- **Ctrl + Shift + F**: Format the code according to the configured standards.

- **Ctrl + D**: Delete the entire current line.

- **Alt + Shift + Up/Down**: Move the current line or selected block up or down.

3. **Refactoring**

- **Alt + Shift + R**: Rename a variable, method, or class.

- **Alt + Shift + M**: Extract selected code into a new method.

- **Alt + Shift + I**: Invert an `if-else`

statement.

4. **Debugging**

- **F5**: Step into the next method call during debugging.

- **F6**: Step over the next statement within the same function.

- **F8**: Resume program execution until the next breakpoint.

5. **Working with Multiple Editors**

- **Ctrl + F6**: Switch between open editors.

- **Ctrl + W**: Close the current editor.

- **Ctrl + Shift + W**: Close all open editors.

Code Organization

Efficient code organization is crucial to ensuring that the project is maintainable and easily understandable by other developers.

Eclipse provides various tools to help keep your code orderly and well-structured.

1. **Packages and Classes**

Java projects in Eclipse are typically organized into **packages**. A package is a folder containing classes and other resources. Organizing code into packages helps keep logical modules and functionalities separate.

For example, a project could be structured as follows:

```
src/
    com.example.main/
        MainClass.java
    com.example.utils/
        UtilityClass.java
```

Each class has a logical location within the project, making navigation and code management easier.

2. **Naming Conventions**

Maintaining consistent naming conventions improves code readability. While Eclipse doesn't enforce conventions, it provides suggestions based on best practices:

- Classes and interfaces: start with an uppercase letter (e.g., `MainClass`, `DataProcessor`).

- Variables and methods: start with a lowercase letter and use camelCase (e.g., `calculateSum`, `userAge`).

- Constants: use all uppercase letters with underscores between words (e.g., `MAX_LENGTH`, `DEFAULT_VALUE`).

3. **Organizing Imports**

Eclipse helps manage **imports** automatically:

- **Ctrl + Shift + O**: Removes unnecessary imports and organizes the existing ones.

This is especially useful when working on large projects with many dependencies.

4. **Javadoc and Comments**

Eclipse makes it easy to add **Javadoc comments** to document your code:

- Typing `/**` followed by **Enter** automatically generates a Javadoc block above a class or method.

Javadoc comments improve code readability and are essential for creating well-structured documentation.

Compiling and Debugging in Eclipse

Compiling and debugging code are essential operations for any developer. Eclipse provides powerful tools to manage the build process and debug applications in a simple and intuitive way.

Compiler Setup

Eclipse uses a **built-in compiler** for most supported languages but also allows the configuration of external compilers. For a Java project, the default compiler is Eclipse's, but you can specify different JDK versions if necessary.

1. **Configuring the JDK**

To configure the JDK version to use in your project:

- Go to **Window > Preferences > Java > Installed JREs**.

- Add a new JRE if it's not already present, and select the JDK directory you wish to use.

- Select the appropriate JDK version for the project.

2. **Configuring Compilation Options**

Each project can have different compilation settings. To access a Java project's compilation settings:

- Right-click the project and select **Properties**.

- Go to the **Java Compiler** section, where you can specify the compiler version, compliance levels, and other compilation options (such as syntax errors and warnings).

Running and Managing Builds

Eclipse automatically handles the build process during development, but you can configure **external builds** or custom builds for complex projects, such as those based on **Maven** or **Gradle**.

1. **Running a Program**

To run a Java program in Eclipse:

- Select the main file containing the `main()` method.

- Click **Run > Run As > Java Application**.

Eclipse will automatically compile and run the project.

2. **Managing Run Configurations**

If you need to configure how your program runs in more detail (e.g., passing arguments or setting environment variables):

- Go to **Run > Run Configurations**.

- Select the existing run configuration or create a new one.

- Here you can configure arguments, environment variables, and other specific parameters.

Debugging Tools

Debugging is one of the most critical parts of software development. Eclipse offers a comprehensive and powerful environment to debug code.

1. **Setting Breakpoints**

A breakpoint is a point in the code where program execution pauses, allowing you to inspect the state of variables and the execution flow:

- To add a breakpoint, click on the left bar next to the code line.

During execution, the program will pause when it reaches the breakpoint, letting you examine the context.

2. **Inspecting Variables**

During debugging, Eclipse provides a detailed view of **local variables** and **fields** in the current context. You can see variable values, modify them on the fly, and navigate through threads.

3. **Controlling Execution Flow**

Eclipse allows you to step through the program:

- **F5 (Step Into)**: Step into the called method.

- **F6 (Step Over)**: Execute the next statement without stepping into methods.

- **F7 (Step Return)**: Execute the current method until its end and return to the caller.

- **F8 (Resume)**: Resume execution until the next breakpoint.

4. **Watch Expressions**

You can add custom expressions to watch during debugging. Go to **Expressions** in the Debug view and add a new expression to monitor how values

change as the program progresses.

Remote Application Debugging

Eclipse also supports remote debugging, allowing you to debug applications running on a remote server or another machine. To configure it:

- Go to **Run > Debug Configurations**.

- Select **Remote Java Application** and configure the remote host and port.

5.Using Git with Eclipse

The integration of Git in Eclipse provides a powerful solution for managing version control directly from the integrated development environment (IDE). Eclipse, through the **EGit** plugin, offers a wide range of tools to interact with both local and remote Git repositories, simplifying operations such as cloning, committing, pushing, pulling, merging, and managing branches. This integration is essential for improving team collaboration and maintaining strict control over software versions.

Git Integration in Eclipse

1. **Installing EGit**

EGit is the plugin that allows the use of Git in Eclipse. In most modern versions of Eclipse, EGit is already included, but if it's not, here's how to install it:

1. Go to **Help > Eclipse Marketplace**.

2. In the search bar, enter "EGit" and press Enter.

3. Find "EGit – Git Integration for Eclipse" and click **Install**.

4. Follow the instructions to complete the installation, and restart Eclipse if prompted.

Once installed, you'll be ready to work with Git directly within Eclipse.

2. **Initial Git Configuration**

Before starting to work with Git in Eclipse, it's important to configure some global Git settings, such as the username and email address, which will be used for commits. Here's how to configure these settings in Eclipse:

1. Go to **Window > Preferences**.

2. In the preferences window, expand the

Team section and select **Git > Configuration**.

3. Click on **Add Entry** and enter:

   - Name: `user.name`

   - Value: Your name

4. Repeat the process to add your email address:

   - Name: `user.email`

   - Value: Your email address

These details will be used for every commit you make through Eclipse.

3. **Git Explorer**

Eclipse includes a view called **Git Repositories**, accessible via **Window > Show View > Other > Git > Git Repositories**. This view allows you to navigate through Git repositories, manage branches, tags, commits, and other common Git operations.

Repository Management

A Git repository is the heart of a versioned project. You can manage both local and remote repositories in Eclipse, and working with Git repositories is greatly simplified through EGit.

1. **Cloning a Remote Repository**

Cloning a remote repository is the most common way to start working on an existing project. Here's how to clone a remote repository using Eclipse:

1. Go to **File > Import**.

2. Select **Git > Projects from Git** and click **Next**.

3. Select **Clone URI** and click **Next**.

4. In the next window, enter the **URI of the remote Git repository**. These details can be

provided by the Git server (e.g., GitHub, GitLab, Bitbucket) and include:

  - **URI**: The link to the Git repository.

  - **Host**: The repository host (e.g., `github.com`).

  - **Repository Path**: The remote repository path.

  - **Authentication**: If the repository requires authentication, enter your credentials.

5. Click **Next**, select the branches you want to clone, and click **Finish**.

After cloning the repository, it will be displayed in the **Git Repositories** view, and you'll be ready to work on the code.

2. **Creating a New Local Repository**

If you're starting a new project and want to version the code with Git, you can create a local repository directly from Eclipse.

1. Go to **File > New > Project** and select the type of project you want to create (e.g., a Java project).

2. Once the project is created, right-click on the project folder in the **Project Explorer** view and select **Team > Share Project**.

3. In the window that opens, select **Git** and click **Next**.

4. In the next screen, you can choose to use an existing Git repository or create a new one. Select **Create a new repository** and choose the directory where the repository will be saved.

5. Click **Finish**.

Your project is now under version control with Git, and you can start tracking the changes you make.

3. **Adding a Remote Repository**

If you have created a local repository and want to link it to a remote repository (e.g., on GitHub or GitLab), follow these steps:

1. In the **Git Repositories** view, right-click on the repository and select **Remotes > Configure Push to Upstream**.

2. Click **Add** and enter the URI of the remote repository.

3. Enter your authentication details (if required).

4. Select the branch you want to push and click **Finish**.

Now the remote repository is linked, and you can perform push and pull operations.

Commit and Push Operations

Once your repository is set up, you can begin committing your local changes and pushing them to the remote repository. Git in Eclipse handles these operations smoothly, making the process intuitive even for less experienced developers.

1. **Adding Files to Version Control**

When you create or modify files in Eclipse, they are not automatically tracked by Git. To add a file to version control:

1. Go to the **Project Explorer** or **Package Explorer** view.

2. Right-click on the file or folder you want to add and select **Team > Add to Index**.

This command performs the equivalent of `git add` and moves the files to Git's **index**, the staging area where files are prepared for commit.

2. **Performing a Commit**

A commit is the operation where you save a "snapshot" of the project, including the files that have been modified in the index.

1. After adding the files to the index, right-click on the project in the **Project Explorer** view and select **Team > Commit**.

2. In the commit window that opens, you can:

   - Select the files you want to include in the commit.

   - Write a meaningful **commit message** that describes the changes.

   - Check the **Amend** option if you want to modify the last commit instead of creating a new one.

3. Click **Commit** to save the changes to the local repository.

3. **Pushing Changes**

Once you have committed your changes locally, you'll need to send them to the remote repository via a push operation.

1. Right-click on the project or repository in the **Git Repositories** view.

2. Select **Team > Push to Upstream**.

3. In the push configuration window, you can review the branch details and the remote repository.

4. Click **Finish** to send the changes to the remote repository.

If the push is successful, the changes will be visible in the remote repository, such as on GitHub or GitLab.

Additional Operations

In addition to commit and push operations, Eclipse with EGit supports several other essential operations for the daily management of a versioned project with Git.

1. **Pulling from the Remote Repository**

The **pull** operation allows you to update

your local repository with changes from the remote repository. Here's how to perform a pull in Eclipse:

1. Right-click on the project or repository in the **Git Repositories** view.

2. Select **Team > Pull**.

3. Eclipse will download the changes from the remote repository and integrate them into your local repository.

If there are conflicts between local and remote changes, Eclipse will notify you and allow you to resolve them.

2. **Creating and Managing Branches**

Branches are one of Git's most powerful features, allowing you to isolate the development of new features or bug fixes. Here's how to create and manage branches in Eclipse:

- **Create a new branch**: Go to **Team > Switch to > New Branch**, enter the name of the new branch, and click **Finish**.

- **Switch to an existing branch**: Go to **Team > Switch to > Branch**, select the branch you want to switch to, and click **Finish**.

- **Merge branches**: To merge changes from one branch to another, go to **Team > Merge** and select the branch you want to merge into the current branch.

The integration of Git in Eclipse through the EGit plugin provides developers with a complete set of tools to manage version control directly from the IDE. From cloning remote repositories to managing commits, push, pull, and branches, Eclipse makes using Git accessible and intuitive, even for those new to distributed version control. With its wide range of features, Eclipse's Git integration facilitates both team collaboration and individual development, keeping the code always under control.

6.Web Development with Eclipse

Eclipse is a powerful integrated development environment (IDE) that supports various languages and frameworks, making it an excellent option for web development. With its integrated tools and plugins, Eclipse provides support for configuring web environments, using integrated servers, and developing web applications. In this guide, we'll explore these aspects in detail, providing examples and best practices to help you successfully start your web project in Eclipse.

Setting Up a Web Environment

1. **Installing Eclipse IDE**

To get started, ensure you have the correct version of Eclipse installed. The **Eclipse IDE for Java EE Developers** is recommended for web development, as it includes the necessary tools and plugins.

Downloading Eclipse

1. Visit the official Eclipse website [eclipse.org](https://www.eclipse.org/).

2. Download the **Eclipse IDE for Java EE Developers** version.

3. Follow the installation instructions for your operating system.

2. **Installing Required Plugins**

Eclipse supports various plugins that can be installed to facilitate web development. Here are some essential plugins:

- **Eclipse Web Developer Tools**: Provides support for HTML, CSS, and JavaScript.

- **Apache Tomcat**: A popular web server for running Java Servlet applications.

- **JSTL (JavaServer Pages Standard Tag Library)**: For JSP management.

To install these plugins:

1. Go to **Help > Eclipse Marketplace**.

2. Search for the desired plugins, select them, and click **Go**.

3. Install the plugins by following the on-screen instructions.

3. **Configuring a Web Project**

After installing the necessary plugins, you can set up a web project. Here's how:

1. Go to **File > New > Dynamic Web Project**.

2. In the dialog box, enter a name for the project (e.g., `MyWebApp`).

3. Select the **Target Runtime** (e.g., Apache Tomcat).

4. Complete the wizard by clicking **Finish**.

This will create a dynamic web project structure, ready for implementation.

4. **Web Project Structure**

A typical web project structure in Eclipse includes the following:

```
MyWebApp/
├── src/
│   └── main/
│       └── java/
│           └── com.example.mywebapp/
├── WebContent/
│   ├── META-INF/
│   ├── WEB-INF/
│   │   └── web.xml
│   └── index.jsp
```

- **src/main/java**: Contains the Java source code.

- **WebContent**: Contains web resources like JSP, HTML, CSS, and images.

- **WEB-INF**: Contains configuration files, including `web.xml` for servlet configuration.

Using Integrated Servers

Eclipse offers the ability to use integrated servers like Apache Tomcat and Jetty, simplifying the process of developing and testing web applications.

1. **Adding a Server to Eclipse**

Here's how to add a Tomcat server to the Eclipse environment:

1. Go to **Window > Show View > Servers**.

2. In the Servers view, right-click and select

74

New > Server.

3. Choose **Apache > Tomcat v9.0 Server** and click **Next**.

4. Specify the Tomcat installation directory on your computer.

5. Add the project (`MyWebApp`) to the list of projects to be published on the server.

6. Click **Finish**.

2. **Starting the Server**

After configuring the server, you can start it directly from Eclipse:

1. In the Servers view, right-click on the server and select **Start**.

2. Eclipse will start the server and open your default browser at the project's URL (usually `http://localhost:8080/MyWebApp`).

3. **Publishing Changes**

When you make changes to the code, Eclipse allows you to publish them to the server without manually restarting it:

1. Save your changes.

2. In the Servers view, right-click on the server and select **Publish**.

Eclipse will automatically update the server with the new resources.

Web Application Development

1. **Creating a Servlet**

Servlets are Java components that handle web requests and responses. Here's how to create a servlet in Eclipse:

1. Right-click the **src/main/java** folder in your project and select **New > Servlet**.

2. Enter the name of the servlet (e.g., `HelloServlet`).

3. Choose the package (e.g., `com.example.mywebapp`).

4. Complete the wizard and click **Finish**.

Here's an example of a simple servlet:

```java
package com.example.mywebapp;

import java.io.IOException;

import javax.servlet.ServletException;

import javax.servlet.annotation.WebServlet;

import javax.servlet.http.HttpServlet;

import javax.servlet.http.HttpServletRequest;

import javax.servlet.http.HttpServletResponse;
```

```java
@WebServlet("/hello")

public class HelloServlet extends HttpServlet
{

    protected void doGet(HttpServletRequest
request, HttpServletResponse response)

        throws ServletException, IOException
{

        response.setContentType("text/html");

        response.getWriter().println("<h1>Hello,
World!</h1>");

    }

}
```

2. **Configuring `web.xml`**

The `web.xml` file in the `WEB-INF` folder is
the configuration file for servlets. To register
the servlet, open the `web.xml` file and add
the following lines:

```xml
<servlet>

    <servlet-name>HelloServlet</servlet-name>

    <servlet-class>com.example.mywebapp.HelloServlet</servlet-class>

</servlet>

<servlet-mapping>

    <servlet-name>HelloServlet</servlet-name>

    <url-pattern>/hello</url-pattern>

</servlet-mapping>
```

3. **Creating a JSP Page**

JavaServer Pages (JSP) are used to create dynamic content. You can create a JSP page in your project by following these steps:

1. Right-click the **WebContent** folder and select **New > JSP File**.

2. Name the file (e.g., `index.jsp`).

3. Add the following code:

```jsp
<%@ page language="java"
contentType="text/html; charset=UTF-8"

    pageEncoding="UTF-8"%>
<!DOCTYPE html>
<html>
<head>
    <title>My Web App</title>
</head>
<body>
    <h1>Welcome to My Web App</h1>
    <a href="hello">Say Hello</a>
</body>
</html>
```

```
```

4. **Testing the Application**

To test the application:

1. Start the Tomcat server as described earlier.

2. Open your browser and go to the URL: `http://localhost:8080/MyWebApp/index.jsp`.

3. Click the "Say Hello" link to invoke the servlet and see the "Hello, World!" message.

5. **Using Web Frameworks**

Eclipse also supports web frameworks such as **Spring** and **JSF (JavaServer Faces)**. You can install the necessary plugins and follow specific guides to integrate these frameworks into your web project.

Example with Spring

To use **Spring MVC**, follow these steps:

1. Add Maven support to your project if you haven't done so already.

2. Add the necessary dependencies to the `pom.xml` file:

```xml
<dependency>
    <groupId>org.springframework</groupId>
    <artifactId>spring-webmvc</artifactId>
    <version>5.3.8</version>
</dependency>
```

3. Create a Spring configuration file and controller classes.

6. **Managing Data Persistence**

If you're developing a web application that

requires data persistence, you can integrate
JPA (Java Persistence API) into your
project:

1. Add the JPA dependencies to your
`pom.xml`:

```xml
<dependency>

<groupId>org.springframework.boot</groupId>

    <artifactId>spring-boot-starter-data-jpa</artifactId>

</dependency>
```

2. Configure the database connection in a
configuration file (e.g.,
`application.properties`).

3. Create JPA entities to map to the database tables and repositories to handle CRUD operations.

7. **Testing the Application**

To ensure your application works correctly, you can write tests using tools such as **JUnit** and **Mockito**. Eclipse supports integrated testing, allowing you to run tests directly from the IDE.

Web development with Eclipse is a powerful and flexible process. With integrated servers, development tools, and support for various frameworks, Eclipse allows you to manage the full lifecycle of an application, from initial setup to deployment. By following the steps outlined in this guide, you will be able to create, test, and deploy web applications successfully. Whether you're working on a simple project or a complex application, Eclipse provides the tools necessary to streamline your development.

7.Android Application Development in Eclipse

Developing Android applications in Eclipse was once a popular approach before the introduction of Android Studio. Although Android Studio is now the official IDE for Android development, Eclipse, along with the ADT (Android Development Tools) plugin, still provides a complete environment for creating and testing Android applications. This guide will explore the steps to set up the Android environment, create a new app, and debug and test the application.

Setting Up the Android Environment

1. **Installing Eclipse**

To begin, you need to have Eclipse installed. Follow these steps:

1. **Download Eclipse**:

- Go to the official Eclipse website: [eclipse.org](https://www.eclipse.org/).

- Choose the **Eclipse IDE for Java Developers** version.

2. **Install Eclipse**:

- Follow the installation instructions for your operating system.

2. **Installing the ADT Plugin**

The ADT plugin allows you to develop Android apps within Eclipse. Here's how to install it:

1. **Open Eclipse**.

2. Go to **Help > Install New Software**.

3. In the window that opens, enter the ADT repository URL:

```

https://dl-ssl.google.com/android/eclipse/
```

```

4. Select the components to install (Android Development Tools) and click **Next**.

5. Follow the instructions to complete the installation and restart Eclipse.

### 3. **Installing Android SDK**

The Android SDK is necessary for app development. You can install it as follows:

1. **Download Android SDK**:

   - Visit the official Android website: [developer.android.com] (https://developer.android.com/studio).

   - Download the standalone SDK.

2. **Configure the SDK in Eclipse**:

   - Go to **Window > Preferences**.

   - Expand the **Android** section and specify the path to the Android SDK.
```

4. **Configuring the Android Emulator**

The Android emulator is a critical tool for testing applications. You can configure it by following these steps:

1. Open the **Android SDK Manager** from Eclipse (Window > Android SDK Manager).

2. Download the necessary system images for the emulators.

3. Create a new AVD (Android Virtual Device) using the AVD Manager, selecting a system image and configuring hardware settings.

Creating a New Android App

1. **Creating the Project**

To create a new Android app in Eclipse, follow these steps:

1. Go to **File > New > Project**.

2. Select **Android Application Project** and click **Next**.

3. Enter the app name (e.g., `MyFirstApp`), the package name (e.g., `com.example.myfirstapp`), and choose the target SDK.

4. Click **Next**.

2. **App Configuration**

After creating the project, Eclipse will ask you to configure the app settings:

1. **Activity**: Select to create a `Blank Activity` and give the main activity a name (e.g., `MainActivity`).

2. **Layout**: You can choose to automatically generate an XML layout.

3. Click **Finish** to complete the project creation.

3. **Project Structure**

Once the project is created, you will have the following structure:

```
MyFirstApp/
├── src/
│    └── com.example.myfirstapp/
│        └── MainActivity.java
├── res/
│    ├── layout/
│    │    └── activity_main.xml
│    ├── mipmap/
│    └── values/
│        └── strings.xml
└── AndroidManifest.xml
```

- **MainActivity.java**: Contains the code for the main activity.

- **activity_main.xml**: The XML layout file.

- **AndroidManifest.xml**: App configuration file.

4. **Writing the Code**

You can now modify `MainActivity.java` to add functionality. Here's a simple example:

```java
package com.example.myfirstapp;


import android.os.Bundle;

import android.widget.TextView;

import androidx.appcompat.app.AppCompatActivity;


public class MainActivity extends
```

```java
AppCompatActivity {

    @Override

    protected void onCreate(Bundle
savedInstanceState) {

        super.onCreate(savedInstanceState);

        setContentView(R.layout.activity_main);


        TextView textView =
findViewById(R.id.textView);

        textView.setText("Hello, Android!");

    }

}
```

In the `activity_main.xml` layout, add a
`TextView`:


```xml
<RelativeLayout
```

```
xmlns:android="http://schemas.android.com/a
pk/res/android"

    android:layout_width="match_parent"

    android:layout_height="match_parent">


    <TextView

        android:id="@+id/textView"

        android:layout_width="wrap_content"

        android:layout_height="wrap_content"

        android:textSize="24sp" />

</RelativeLayout>
```
```

## Debugging and Testing Android Apps


### 1. **Debugging the App**

Debugging is a critical part of Android app development. Eclipse provides debugging tools that you can use:
```

1. **Set a breakpoint**: Open `MainActivity.java`, click on the line where you want to pause execution (e.g., inside the `onCreate` method), and select **Toggle Breakpoint**.

2. **Run the debug**: Go to **Run > Debug As > Android Application**. Eclipse will launch the emulator or a connected device and stop at the breakpoint.

2. **Inspecting Variables**

Once paused at a breakpoint, you can inspect local variables and see their current state in the **Variables** view. You can also modify variable values to test different scenarios.

3. **Testing the App**

There are various ways to test your Android app:

A. **Testing on Emulator**

You can test the app directly on the Android emulator. If you've already set up an AVD, you can run the app just like you would on a physical device.

1. Ensure the emulator is running.

2. Go to **Run > Run As > Android Application** to install and launch the app on the emulator.

B. **Testing on a Physical Device**

To test the app on a physical Android device:

1. Ensure the device has **USB Debugging** enabled (Settings > Developer Options > USB Debugging).

2. Connect the device to your computer via USB.

3. Eclipse should recognize the device and allow you to run the app on it.

4. **Writing Automated Tests**

Eclipse supports writing automated tests using **JUnit**. You can create unit tests for your classes and methods. Here's how to do it:

1. Create a new test class:

   - Right-click on the `src` folder and select **New > Class**.

   - Name the test class (e.g., `MainActivityTest`).

2. Write a simple test:

```java
package com.example.myfirstapp;

import org.junit.Test;
import static org.junit.Assert.*;
```

```java
public class MainActivityTest {

    @Test

    public void testExample() {

        assertTrue(true);

    }

}
```
```

3. Run the test:

   - Right-click the test class and select **Run As > JUnit Test**.

### 5. **Using the Android Test Framework**

To test the user interface, you can use the Android Testing Framework. You can write UI tests using tools like Espresso or UI Automator.

Here's an example of a UI test using Espresso:
```

```java
import androidx.test.espresso.Espresso;

import
androidx.test.ext.junit.runners.AndroidJUnit4;

import androidx.test.rule.ActivityTestRule;

import org.junit.Rule;

import org.junit.Test;

import org.junit.runner.RunWith;


import static
androidx.test.espresso.action.ViewActions.click;

import static
androidx.test.espresso.assertion.ViewAssertions.matches;

import static
androidx.test.espresso.matcher.ViewMatchers.withId;

import static
androidx.test.espresso.matcher.ViewMatchers.
```

withText;

```java
@RunWith(AndroidJUnit4.class)
public class MainActivityTest {
    @Rule
    public ActivityTestRule<MainActivity>
    activityRule =

        new
    ActivityTestRule<>(MainActivity.class);


    @Test
    public void testTextView() {

Espresso.onView(withId(R.id.textView)).chec
k(matches(withText("Hello, Android!")));
    }
}
```
```
```

6. **Optimizing App Performance**

Optimizing the performance of Android applications is crucial. Use tools like **Android Profiler** to monitor memory usage, CPU utilization, and network traffic while the app is running. This tool helps you identify bottlenecks and improve user experience.

Although Android Studio is now the standard, Eclipse with ADT still offers a valid environment for beginners. This guide has covered setting up the Android environment, creating a new app, and debugging and testing the application.

By mastering these tools and techniques, you'll be able to develop and optimize Android applications effectively. With continuous practice and exploration, you'll deepen your knowledge and create more complex and functional apps.

8.Appendices: Useful Commands, Troubleshooting Common Issues, and Eclipse Glossary

This appendix provides a collection of valuable information to optimize the use of Eclipse, address common issues, and understand technical terminology. It is designed as a quick reference resource for developers at all levels.

Useful Eclipse Commands

Eclipse is a powerful and versatile IDE, and knowing its commands can significantly boost productivity. Below are some useful commands and keyboard shortcuts.

1. **Navigation**

- **Open Project Explorer**: `Alt + Shift + Q`, then press `P`.

- **Search Files**: `Ctrl + H` to open the search window.

- **Navigate to Definition**: `F3` to jump to the definition of the selected class or method.

- **Go Back**: `Alt + Left Arrow` to return to the previous location.

- **Go Forward**: `Alt + Right Arrow` to move forward.

2. **Code Editing**

- **Format Code**: `Ctrl + Shift + F` to format the source code according to style settings.

- **Comment/Uncomment Line**: `Ctrl + /` to comment or uncomment the selected line.

- **Organize Imports**: `Ctrl + Shift + O` to automatically import necessary classes.

3. **Running and Debugging**

- **Run Application**: `Ctrl + F11` to run the application.

- **Debug Application**: `F11` to run the app in debug mode.

- **Toggle Breakpoint**: `Ctrl + Shift + B` to toggle a breakpoint at the current line.

4. **Project Management**

- **New Project**: `Ctrl + N` to open the new project dialog.

- **Import Existing Project**: `File > Import...` to import an existing project.

- **Export Project**: `File > Export...` to export the project in various formats, such as JAR or ZIP.

5. **Search and Replace**

- **Search Within a File**: `Ctrl + F` to search inside the currently open file.

- **Search in the Entire Project**: `Ctrl + Shift + F` to search all project files.

- **Replace**: `Ctrl + H` to open the search and replace window.

6. **View Management**

- **Close a View**: `Ctrl + F7` to cycle through open views.

- **Restore a Closed View**: `Window > Show View` to reopen a closed view.

Troubleshooting Common Issues

During the use of Eclipse, you may encounter various issues. Below are solutions to some of the most common problems.

1. **Performance Issues**

- **Symptom**: Eclipse is slow or freezes.

- **Solution**:

  - Ensure you have enough available RAM. Increase the memory allocated to Eclipse by modifying the `eclipse.ini` file:

    ```ini
    -Xms512m

    -Xmx2048m
    ```

  - Disable unnecessary plugins in **Help > About Eclipse IDE > Installation Details**.

2. **Compilation Issues**

- **Symptom**: Compilation errors appear even for correct code.

- **Solution**:

  - Ensure the JDK is correctly configured in Eclipse preferences (**Window > Preferences > Java > Installed JREs**).

- Clean the project using `Project > Clean`.

3. **Import Errors**

- **Symptom**: Classes cannot be found during import.

- **Solution**:

  - Verify that the project's classpath is correctly set (**Right-click on the project > Properties > Java Build Path**).

  - Ensure that necessary libraries are included in the project.

4. **Debugging Problems**

- **Symptom**: Breakpoints do not stop the execution or the debugger does not start.

- **Solution**:

  - Check if breakpoints are active (they should appear as solid circles).

- Run the app in debug mode and ensure the code was compiled with debugging information.

5. **General Error Messages**

- **Symptom**: General error messages appear when starting Eclipse.
- **Solution**:

  - Check the Eclipse logs in `workspace/.metadata/.log` for detailed error information.

  - Try launching Eclipse with a new workspace.

Eclipse Glossary

This glossary includes common terms used in Eclipse and in software development in general.

1. **IDE (Integrated Development Environment)**

A software application that provides tools for developers to write, test, and debug code.

2. **Plugin**

A software module that adds functionality to a main application. Eclipse supports a wide range of plugins to extend its capabilities.

3. **Workspace**

The area in Eclipse where projects and user settings are stored. You can have multiple workspaces and switch between them.

4. **Project**

A collection of files, configurations, and settings used to develop a software application within Eclipse.

5. **Build Path**

The build path specifies where Eclipse looks for classes and libraries during code compilation. It includes source directories, external JARs, and libraries.

6. **Classpath**

A variable that tells Java where to find classes and packages during program execution.

7. **Breakpoints**

Points in the code where execution halts to allow debugging. You can set breakpoints in Eclipse by clicking on the left margin of the code line.

8. **Refactoring**

The process of restructuring source code to improve its structure and readability without altering its external behavior.

9. **Version Control**

A system that tracks changes to source code over time, allowing developers to revert to previous versions and facilitating team collaboration.

10. **Syntax Highlighting**

A feature that highlights the syntax of code based on its structure and type, making it easier to read and understand.

11. **JRE (Java Runtime Environment)**

The environment required to run Java applications. It includes the Java Virtual

Machine (JVM) and necessary libraries.

12. **JDK (Java Development Kit)**

A package that provides tools and libraries for developing Java applications. It includes the JRE and development tools like the compiler.

13. **MVC (Model-View-Controller)**

An architectural pattern used in software development to separate the application logic (model), user interface (view), and interaction control (controller).

14. **XML (eXtensible Markup Language)**

A markup language used to represent data in a way that is readable by both humans and machines. It is often used for configuration in Eclipse and Android applications.

15. **API (Application Programming Interface)**

A set of rules and specifications that allows different applications to communicate with each other. In Eclipse, API often refers to third-party libraries or Java functionalities.

This appendix provides a set of tools and resources to enhance your experience using Eclipse. Knowing useful commands, having a strategy for resolving common issues, and understanding technical jargon can make the development process smoother and more efficient. Whether you are a beginner or an experienced developer, this information serves as a quick guide to tackling everyday challenges in software development.

Index

8.Appendices: Useful Commands, Troubleshooting Common Issues, and Eclipse Glossary pg.102